Friction

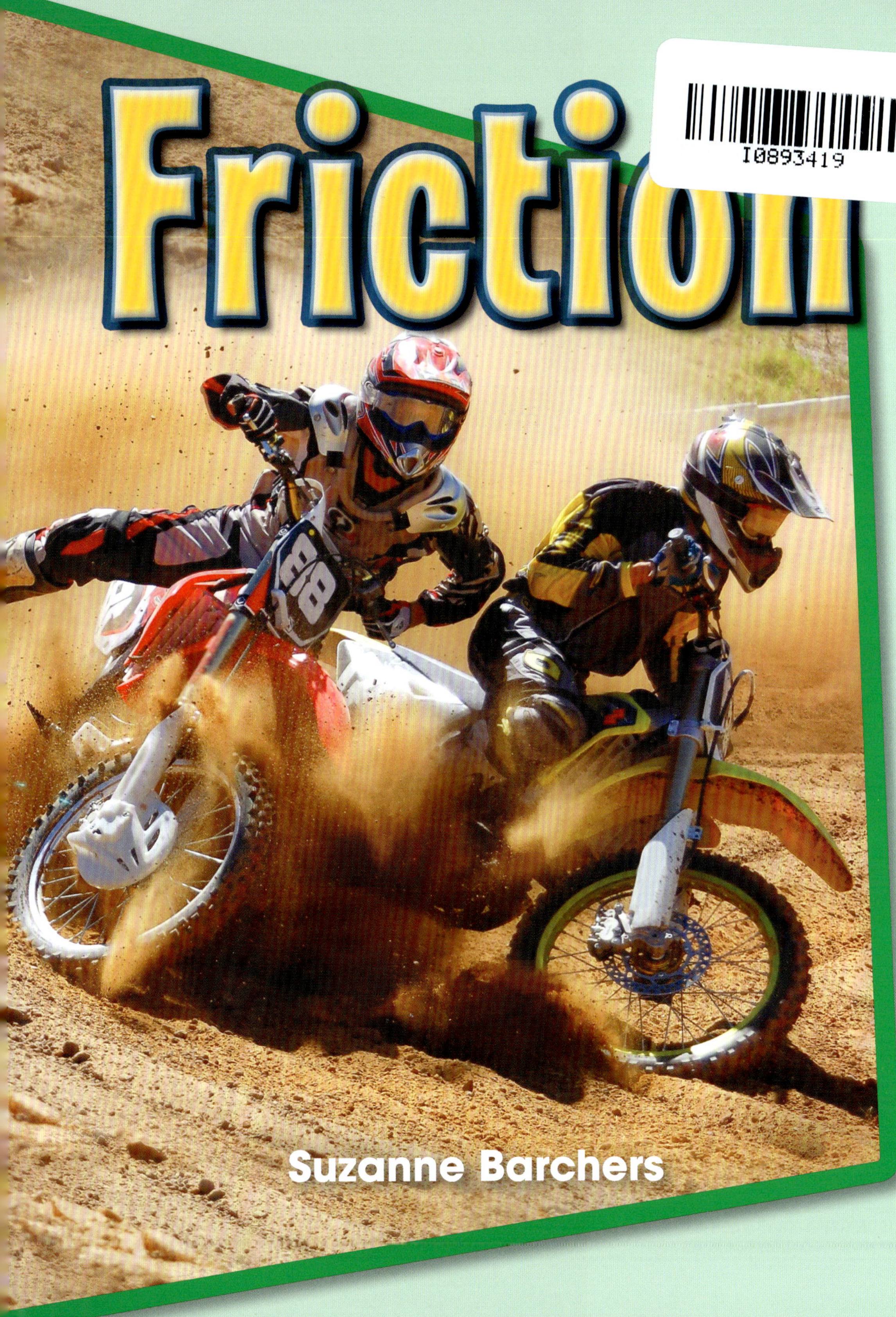

Suzanne Barchers

Consultants

Sally Creel, Ed.D.
Curriculum Consultant

Leann Iacuone, M.A.T., NBCT, ATC
Riverside Unified School District

Image Credits: p.18 Allesalltag Bildagent/age fotostock; p.25 Blend Images/Alamy; p.24 Robert Anton Iuhas/Alamy; p.16 (left) Bettmann/Corbis; p.32 Hillary Dunlap & Stephanie Reid-McGinley; p.9 Na tivestock/ Getty Images; pp.12 (bottom left), 17 (both), 20 iStock; p.15 (left) Muskegon Area Sports; p.11 (bottom) Cheryl Power/Science Source; pp.28–29 (illustrations) J.J. Rudisill; all other images from Shutterstock.

Library of Congress Cataloging-in-Publication Data

Barchers, Suzanne I., author.
Friction / Suzanne Barchers ; consultant, Sally Creel, Ed.D., curriculum consultant, Leann Iacuone, M.A.T., NBCT, ATC Riverside Unified School District, Jill Tobin, California Teacher of the Year semi-finalist Burbank Unified School District.
pages cm
Summary: "When you ride a bike, what makes you stop? Friction. There are different types of friction that help us do things. Even your fingertips use friction to help you can hold things!"— Provided by publisher.
Audience: K to grade 3.
Includes index.
ISBN 978-1-4807-4606-0 (pbk.)
ISBN 978-1-4807-5073-9 (ebook)
1. Friction—Juvenile literature.
2. Force and energy—Juvenile literature. I. Title.
QC197.B36 2015
531.4—dc23
2014014113

Teacher Created Materials
5301 Oceanus Drive
Huntington Beach, CA 92649-1030
http://www.tcmpub.com

ISBN 978-1-4807-4606-0

Printed in China

Table of Contents

Feel the Force!

Did you ride a bike this week? Maybe you went skating or rode a scooter or a skateboard. Each time you used a brake or your foot to stop, you used an important force. That force is called *friction*.

When you move, you use energy. Friction slows this energy. Because of friction, you can't roll on your bike forever. Friction may be the most important force of all. Read on, and then *you* can decide.

Friction keeps this girl in one spot.

This boy is using energy.

Friction in Action

Friction has many purposes. Without it, the world would be a slippery place!

Moving Along

Friction happens whenever two things touch or rub against each other. You counted on friction when you got up this morning, even if you didn't know it. Your blanket stayed in place when you made your bed. And without friction, your socks would be down around your ankles!

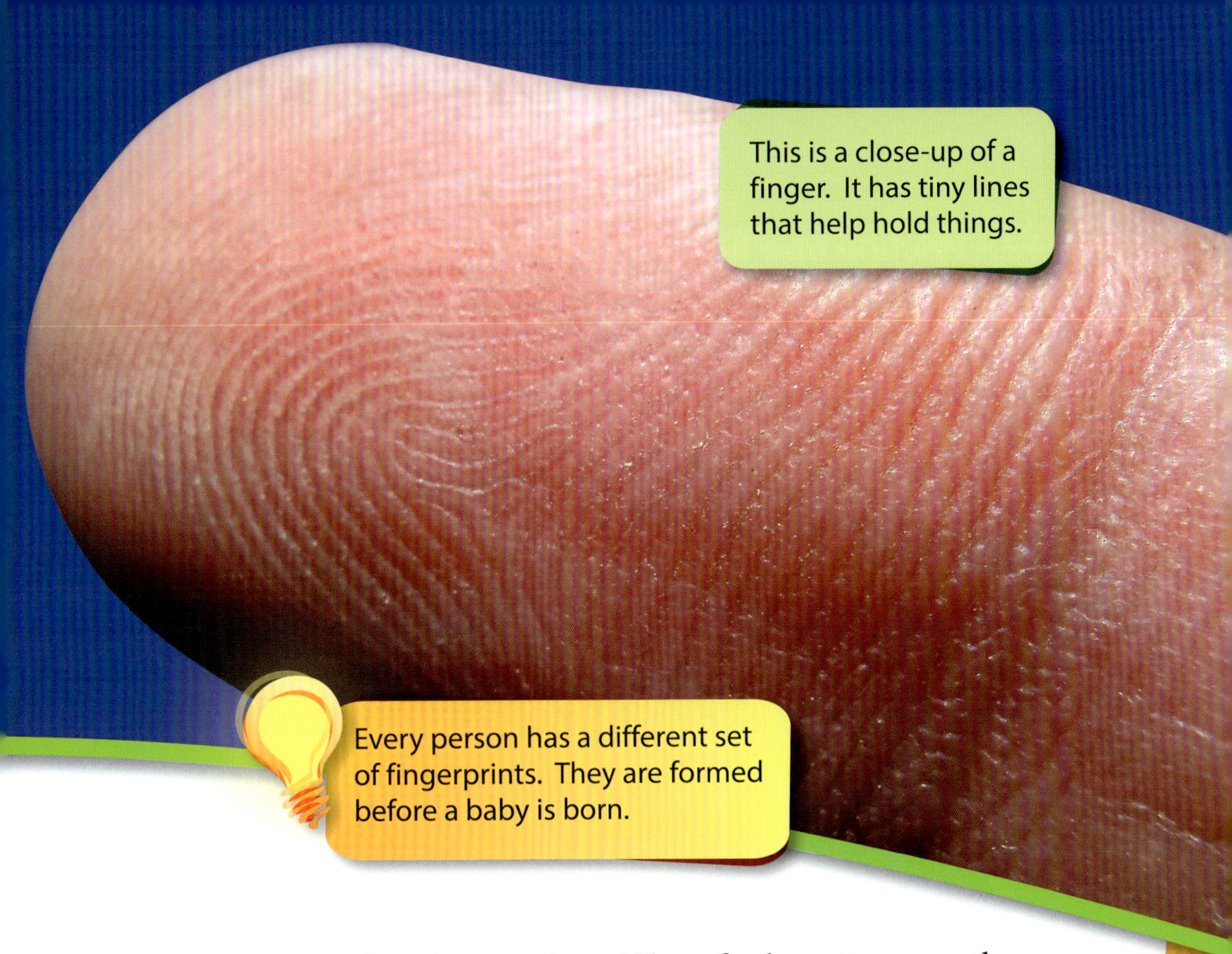

This is a close-up of a finger. It has tiny lines that help hold things.

Every person has a different set of fingerprints. They are formed before a baby is born.

Rub your hands together. They feel pretty smooth, right? Rub them faster and they get warm. That heat (a kind of energy) comes from friction. Your hands aren't perfectly smooth, so the bumps and lines on them rub together and cause friction.

On Fire!

Friction also helps people make fire. People learned to make fire thousands of years ago. They made fire with simple materials, friction, and a lot of energy!

The first people made nests of dry grass and leaves. They placed a tree branch in a notch on a piece of wood. They rolled the branch between their hands. After a lot of work, the dry grass and leaves started to glow. The people blew gently and had fire.

More Fire

Matches also need friction to start a fire. That is why adults need to drag them along the side of a matchbox.

This man shows how people made fire long ago.

Never start a fire without safe conditions, adult help, and permission.

Get a Grip

Friction doesn't just help you make fire. Your fingerprints and tennis shoes use friction, too. The ridges on your fingers help you hold a pen or a ball. The ridges on the bottom of your shoes help you grip the floor. Hiking boots have deeper ridges for better **traction**.

Flies and some reptiles seem to walk anywhere, even on glass! Their feet look smooth. But they have many hairs used for gripping on the bottoms of their feet. And those hairs have some sticky stuff that adds to their traction.

Sticking Together

Traction helps things stick. You want your shoes to have good traction so you don't slip.

This is a close-up of a fly's foot.

Friction at Play

Friction helps us when we play. There are many things we can do because friction exists.

Get in the Game!

Look at these sports shoes. They have cleats, which are metal or rubber bumps. Cleats increase friction to help keep players from falling. Do you play baseball, soccer, or football? Do you run track? Then you know how important good traction is when running.

However, some athletes don't use shoes with cleats. Rock climbers use shoes that help their feet grip rocks. And they may wear fingerless gloves for better grip. Rock climbers put friction to work so they can have fun!

Rock climbers use traction to hold onto rocks.

Smooth Players

For some sports, players don't want very much friction. Ice skaters want smooth, sharp blades. Really fast skaters heat the ice and melt it with their blades. The melted ice speeds them up even more! Snowboarders and skiers put wax on their boards to reduce friction. They want to move smoothly and quickly across the snow. When it's time to stop, they twist and turn to slow down.

This snowboarder pushes her board forward to slow down.

For other sports, gear is built for speed *and* for using friction. In-line skates have brakes built in. Some skateboards have braking systems, too.

These in-line skates have brakes in the back.

An Early Snowboard

Sherman Poppen joined two skis to make a new toy. Friction helps the Snurfer slide downhill at the right speed.

Rolling Along

Do you use a backpack to carry your books? Set it on the floor. It doesn't move. Try dragging it along the floor a few feet. It moves, but it feels heavy. Now, try putting your books in a rolling backpack. It's much easier to move, right?

Static friction holds things in place, such as a backpack on the floor. When you drag the backpack, you use **sliding friction**. Your backpack moves, but there is a lot of drag. With the use of wheels, the friction is reduced. This is called **rolling friction**.

Ancient Egyptians used rolling friction to move huge stones into place. They did this by rolling the stones on top of logs.

Rolling friction makes a heavy backpack move easily.

Drag

Drag is a force. It slows moving things. The more drag there is, the harder it is to move something.

This backpack has sliding friction because it is moving on the ground.

Friction at Work

Friction helps us get the job done!

Feel the Heat

Machines get hot because of friction. All the moving parts rub against one another. The friction from this rubbing can make the temperature climb. This can cause many problems!

Oil is used in cars and trucks to reduce friction. Water is used to cool many kinds of machines. The moving parts of your bike need to be oiled once in a while. Using the right **lubricant** helps a machine last longer.

Bike Right

You can find the right bike oil at a bike shop. Your bike will last longer with the right care.

Oil helps this engine run smoothly.

Shaping Up

You wait at the starting line of a race. You hear someone yell, "Go!" and you take off running. As you run faster, you feel the air against your skin and clothes. It feels like wind, but it's not a windy day. What you feel is a kind of friction called **air resistance.**

Air pushes against these kids as they run.

Look at the pictures of the jet fighter and the blimp. Which one has less air resistance? Jets and blimps are designed to slice through the air. Race cars are also designed with smooth, sleek lines to reduce friction. Cars, on the other hand, need good tire traction. It's safer if they don't go too fast.

This speedboat can move quickly through the water because of its shape.

Water Power

You can study **water resistance** the next time you take a bath. Find a toy boat and move it sideways through the water. It won't move as quickly as when you move the pointed end through the water.

Boats face two challenges—water and air resistance. A speedboat has a sleek shape to help reduce water and air resistance. So does a canoe. A barge has a different design. It is built for moving big loads, not for speed.

Water at Work

Water acts as a lubricant on a water slide. It decreases friction between your skin and the slide.

This boat cannot move as quickly as a speedboat because of water resistance.

A Shocking Idea!

Do you ever walk on carpet in your socks? Do you get a shock once in a while? The friction between your socks and the carpet makes **static electricity**. This is the kind of electricity that collects on the surface of things and may cause a shock. Since friction is everywhere, why not put that friction to work?

Inventors are working on just that. They have made tiny **generators** (JEN-uh-rey-ters) with parts that rub. They work a lot like your socks on the carpet. The parts that rub make energy. One day, this invention may be used in cell phones. Just moving around will charge the battery!

The friction between the slide and this boy's hair make static electricity.

Lightning is a form of static electricity. But it is much stronger than the small shocks that we feel when we touch a doorknob.

Big Ideas

Friction is everywhere. But could you imagine a world without it? Everything would slip and slide! Cars would glide down the street. You would not be able to hold your pencil. There would be no grip or friction. Buildings would fall apart. And sports teams would slide down the fields.

Ice is slippery because there isn't much friction.

What do you think? Is friction the most important force? If you have ever skidded on an icy road, then you know how important friction is!

This car is sliding because there is not enough friction.

Let's Do Science!

Which surface has more friction? See for yourself!

What to Get

- different surfaces (carpet, wood, aluminum foil, waxed paper, or sandpaper)
- long, sturdy rubber band
- ruler
- shoe

What to Do

1. Cut the rubber band so it is one long piece. Tie one end to the shoe and place the shoe on the floor.

2. Stretch the end of the rubber band until it is tight, but don't pull so hard that the shoe moves. Measure the length of the stretched rubber band.

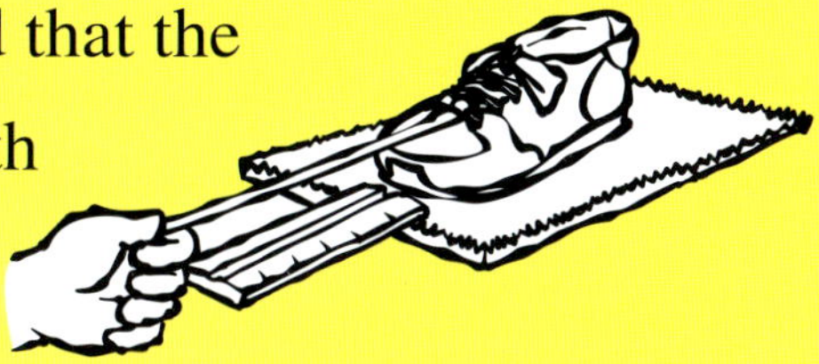

3. Write the length on a chart like the one on the right. Repeat with different surfaces. Look at your chart. Which surface has the most friction?

surface	length
carpet	
wood	
aluminum foil	
wax paper	

Glossary

air resistance—the drag on something caused by moving through air

generators—machines that make electricity

lubricant—something that helps machine parts to be slippery and move more smoothly

rolling friction—the force that slows energy when something is rolled on wheels

sliding friction—the force that slows energy when something is being slid

static electricity—electricity that collects on the surface of things instead of flowing as a current

static friction—the force that prevents something from moving

traction—the force that causes a moving thing to stick against the surface it is moving along

water resistance—the drag on something caused by moving through water

Index

Your Turn!

Friction Challenge

Amaze your friends with this trick! You will need two thick paperback books. Leaf the two books together as shown in the picture. There is a lot of friction because of the many pages touching each other. Challenge your friends to pull them apart!